WRITTEN BY

ODILE BRÉAUD, SYLVIE ASSATHIANY,
JOELLE BUSUTTIL, ANNE DE HENNING,
CHANTAL HENRY-BIÉBAUB, LAURENCE OTTEINHEIMER,
BERNARD PLANCHE, PENNY STANLEY-BAKER

COVER DESIGN BY
STEPHANIE BLUMENTHAL

TRANSLATED AND ADAPTED BY
PAULA SCHANILEC AND ROSEMARY WALLNER

PUBLISHED BY CREATIVE EDUCATION
123 South Broad Street, Mankato, Minnesota 56001
Creative Education is an imprint of The Creative Company

Library of Congress Cataloging-in-Publication Data
[Enfants du monde. English]
Cultures of the world / by Odile Bréaud, et al.
translated by Paula Schanilec and Rosemary Wallner.
(Creative Discoveries)
Includes index.
Summary: Describes the surroundings, daily life, traditions, and customs of people living all around the world.
ISBN: 0-88682-957-7
1. Civilization, Modern—1950—Juvenile literature.   2. Ethnology—Juvenile literature.
3. Manners and customs—Juvenile literature.   4. Human geography.
[1. Human geography.   2. Civilization, Modern,—20th century.   3. Ethnology.
4. Manners and customs.]   I. Bréaud, Odile.   II. Title.   III. Series.
CB429.B7413   1999
909.82'5—dc21   97-22766
First edition

2 4 6 8 9 7 5 3 1

CULTURES OF THE WORLD

CONTENTS

EUROPE	4
NORTH AMERICA	10
CENTRAL AND SOUTH AMERICA	16
AFRICA	24
ASIA	32
AUSTRALASIA	48
TROPICAL ISLANDS	52
GREENLAND	56
EXPLORE AND PLAY	63
GLOSSARY	70
INDEX	74

CREATIVE EDUCATION

Europe—a small, crowded continent . . .

Would you like to travel around the world? To begin with, here is Europe. If you look at a map of the world, you can see that the continents of Europe and Asia form a single, vast territory unbroken by seas or deserts. Some countries, like Russia, are partly in Europe and partly in Asia. The name Europe comes from Europa, the heroine of a Greek legend. Zeus, king of the gods, fell in love with her and carried her to an island in the Mediterranean Sea. European civilization was born on the near shores.

More than 500 million people live in the 47 countries that make up Europe. That's a lot for such a small area! But the population of Europe is not increasing as fast as the rest of the world's population.

Twelve European countries are united in the European Union, or E.U.

Many people set sail from Europe to settle in other countries.

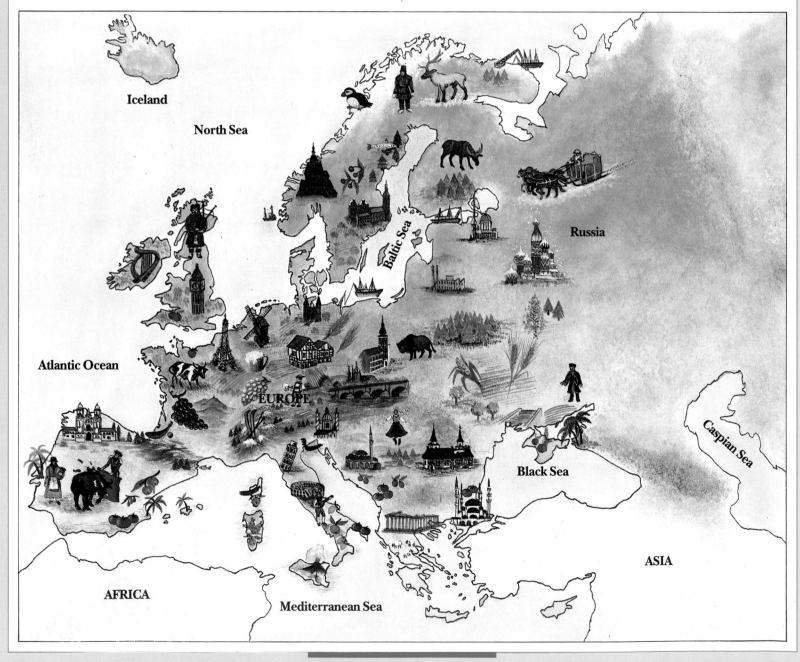

Iceland

North Sea

Baltic Sea

Russia

Atlantic Ocean

EUROPE

Caspian Sea

Black Sea

ASIA

AFRICA

Mediterranean Sea

In Norway, mountains run straight into the sea in fjords.

The coast of western Europe, beaten by the Atlantic Ocean.

Most of Europe has a temperate climate, which means that it is rarely too cold or too hot. Few areas are uninhabitable. Of course, people who make their homes near the Arctic Circle don't live in the same way as those on the Mediterranean Coast! In the extreme north, in Norway and Finland, winter lasts for seven or eight months. The Baltic Sea freezes over. At the same time, in the south, orange trees bear fruit.

On the shores of the Atlantic Ocean, summer and winter are similar. Both are mild and often rainy. This is the climate of Ireland, Great Britain, and the west of France. These areas are green and grassy.

In Central Europe, in Poland, Hungary, the Czech Republic, and Slovakia, the climate is continental, which means that winters are cold and summers are hot.

A southern European landscape, under the blazing sun.

The high, rocky peaks of the Carpathians in Central Europe.

What are houses like in Europe? They vary from country to country, and even from region to region.

In Greece, to keep out the heat and brilliant sunshine of summer, the houses have tiny windows and thick walls painted bright white. Every spring, people whitewash their homes in preparation for the coming summer. White reflects the heat and the house stays cool inside.

Windmills, with sails or wooden blades, aren't just used to grind flour. In the Netherlands, they drive pumps that draw water through the canals. In Greece, they are still used to press oil out of olives.

North of Europe, in Scandinavia, great forests of pine and birch trees still cover huge areas.

Houses there are built of wood, often painted bright red or yellow. In the west of Europe, in Brittany and Normandy in France and in southwest England, a hard rock called granite is found in huge outcrops. It is easy to recognize because it shines in the rain. Here many houses are made of granite.

Red roofs and gray roofs
In the south, roofs are usually covered with red clay tiles that have been fired in a kiln. Mountain chalets are protected by slate, a heavy rock that breaks into fine slivers. Slate roofs resist violent winds well.

In Mediterranean countries, the markets open first thing in the morning while the air is still cool and fresh.

Customs, clothing, and ways of life differ from one place to another too. In Europe, only the British and the Irish drive on the left side of the road!

Mainland Europe measures its goods in meters, kilos, and liters, using the metric system. Great Britain is now gradually moving toward the metric system too.

Because of the heat, Italians and Spaniards take a *siesta,* or rest, in the middle of the day. Shops close until four or five o'clock, then stay open late into the night, when the air is cool and pleasant. The evening is also the time to go for a stroll in southern Europe. This evening walk is called the *paseo* in Spain, the *passeggiata* in Italy. People wander up and down in the shade of the boulevards, greeting friends and exchanging gossip.

Every country in Europe has its own language. Some have more than one. Many of these languages are similar to one another because they share the same Latin, Anglo-Saxon, or Slav roots.

In many parts of Great Britain, milk is delivered to people's doorstep every morning.

The canals of Amsterdam, in the Netherlands, reflect the gables of the brick houses.

In France, there is a bakery in every village. Here the people buy fresh bread every day, early in the morning.

Some celebrations take place all over Europe; others are restricted to a single country. In France, July 14 is Bastille Day, commemorating the French Revolution. In London, on the Queen's official birthday, there is the Trooping of the Color. Christians across Europe celebrate Easter and Christmas; Jews observe Yom Kippur and Hanukkah; and Muslims fast for Ramadan.

Shepherds on mountain pastures high in the Alps and the Pyrenees still wear traditional clothes.

Dancer from Andalusia, in Spain

Hungarian boy

Swedish costume for the festival of St. Lucia

Eggs, flying bells, and a bunny— it must be Easter! Did you know that in France, children believe that Easter eggs are left in the garden by bells that fly from Rome? In Great Britain, Germany, and Austria, they are brought by an Easter bunny that hops around with a basket full of eggs under his arm. In Orthodox Christian countries like Russia and Bulgaria, people paint eggs at Easter.

In Europe, people begin celebrating Christmas on December 6. The children of Belgium and some parts of Germany don't have to wait until December 25, Christmas Day, to receive presents. St. Nicholas comes to visit them and give them gifts on December 6, dressed as a bishop.

In Scandinavia, the holidays begin on December 13, the festival of St. Lucia. In darkest of winter, they celebrate the Festival of Light. The youngest girl in the house wakes up everyone and gives them oranges and sweets.

Young Italians wait eagerly for January 6, the Day of the Kings, when they are visited by "Befana," an old fairy godmother who brings them toys.

| Camembert, France | Quark, Germany | Parmesan, Italy | Manchego, Spain | Gorgonzola, Italy | Double Gloucester, England | Tilsit, Germany |

These days, most people in Europe have enough to eat. This hasn't always been true. In the Middle Ages, for example, food shortages and famines killed thousands. Even today, some countries have problems feeding all of their people. In parts of Central and Eastern Europe, the store shelves are often empty. People have to stand in lines for hours just to buy a loaf of bread.

Have you tasted any of these dishes? Here are some Dutch cheese and *broodjes* (bread rolls); stuffed vine leaves and kebabs from Greece; a French *poteé* (hot pot) with a *baguette* (bread stick); mussels and chips (French fries) from Belgium; roll-mops (herrings) from

To each his own . . . every country has specialties. In Germany, the variety of breads is endless; they are made with every sort of cereal. Italy is home of pasta and is the best place for coffee. France is well known for its wine, and Britain is renowned for its puddings. Nearly every country has its own kind of cheese: Swiss from Switzerland, Gouda from the Netherlands, and Brie from France.

Denmark; Spanish *paella* (a rice and seafood dish); cold meats, sausages, pretzels, and sauerkraut from Germany; a British breakfast of porridge, bacon, and eggs; spaghetti and pizza from Italy, and baked cod from Portugal.

North America used to be called the New World.

To the west of Europe, across the Atlantic Ocean, lies North America. Its first inhabitants came from Asia more than 20,000 years ago. Over the centuries they split into tribes, each with its own customs and traditions. Across the untamed land, they farmed, hunted, and fished. During the 16th century the first Europeans came to North America. Because they thought this unknown land was the Indies, they called the native peoples Indians.

Persecuted for their religious beliefs or tired of living in poverty, many Europeans went to start a new life in North America. The first permanent colony was Jamestown, Virginia, begun in 1607.

At first they settled on the coast, but soon they began to explore the interior in search of new land to settle and farm. Settlers headed west in groups of wagons. It was a dangerous journey that took many lives.

Once they had found a place to build their homesteads, pioneers raised cattle herds, grew crops, or started businesses.

Soon the settlements threatened the survival of the Native Americans, and bitter battles were fought as the native tribes struggled to keep their lands. Eventually the Native Americans were forced to abandon their traditional way of life and move to small reservations (often of poor land) set aside by the government.

Canada, a land of forests and a million lakes

Across the north of North America lies Canada, a huge country, bigger than its neighbor, the United States, but with only about one-eighth of the population. Most of the land is covered in lakes and forests. Canada's forests provide nearly half of the world's wood and countless tons of pulp for making paper. Summers are hot and winters are bitterly cold. The big, bustling cities are all near rivers and lakes in the milder south.

In spring it is time to collect the sap of maple trees. Canadians boil the sap to make maple syrup. The maple leaf, the symbol of Canada, is found on the flag.

Canada has two official languages, French and English. Many people are immigrants and speak a variety of languages.

If polar bears in the far north of Canada don't find enough to eat during the summer, they come into towns and raid garbage cans.

Fifty states: both united and separate

To own a home is part of the "American Dream."

In the United States, there are about as many cars as adults.

Children help at home by doing chores around the house.

Postal trucks deliver mail daily.

The 50 stars on the U.S. flag represent the states. Each state has its own laws and its own capital, but they are bound together under the federal government. Citizens must obey both state and federal laws. The capital of the United States of America is in Washington, in the District of Columbia, which is not in any state.

In many classrooms, students and teachers pledge allegiance to the flag each morning.

From the Atlantic Coast to the Pacific Coast, people live the American way their own way. Native Americans are now a small minority of the U.S. population. Most people are descendants of immigrants who came from all over the world. Though Americans share interstate highways, fast food restaurants, TV stations, national holidays, and a great many things, many also follow their own cultural traditions. In large cities, you can find nearly every kind of ethnic food imaginable.

Children in the United States

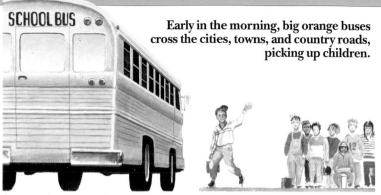

Early in the morning, big orange buses cross the cities, towns, and country roads, picking up children.

American schools are everywhere: in city neighborhoods and busy downtowns, on the edges of sprawling suburbs, in the middle of small towns.

Many children ride a bus to school; others walk or ride a bike, and the school patrol helps them cross the street.

Some children take lunch boxes filled with sandwiches and fruit to school. Others eat hot lunches provided by their school's cafeteria. Many schools across the country also serve students breakfast before class.

American children drink more milk than children of other cultures do. It is often served at every meal of the day.

In the United States and Canada, ice hockey is a popular winter sport. In the summer, children play baseball in parks and yards.

Halloween is when the witches and goblins come out. Of course, the witches and goblins are children wearing costumes. Dressing up for Halloween and "trick or treating" is a U.S. custom.

Jack-o'-lanterns carved from pumpkins keep an eye on the ghostly parade all night long.

In the United States, everything is big.

In the summer, some families take a vacation with their campers or tents to explore the huge natural parks of the American West.

Alaska, the largest U.S. state, is on the northwest coast of Canada.

This immense country includes every habitat you can imagine, from scorching deserts to glistening ice fields.

Pacific Ocean

The state of Hawaii is made up of a chain of 130 islands.

Great Lakes

Mexico

Gulf of Mexico

Atlantic Ocean

The Pacific Coast has thousands of miles of rocky shores and sandy beaches. In the northwest, most of the beaches are deserted.

In Arizona, where the Navaho people live on reservations, huge islands of stone jut out of the red rock of the desert.

The White House, in Washington, D.C., is where the U.S. President lives and works.

The capital of the United States is named after George Washington. He had fought for independence from the British and became the first president in 1789. Every four years, U.S. citizens vote for a new president.

New York is the biggest, busiest city. It is a bustling center of banks, museums, and theaters. Wide streets run in straight lines up and down the crowded island of Manhattan. Skyscrapers almost hide the sky from view.

San Francisco, on the Pacific Coast, is built on 43 hills.

South and Central America, where so many races meet

The lower part of the American continent stretches from Mexico in the north to Tierra del Fuego at the southern tip. The people here speak Spanish or, in Brazil, Portuguese. Many Central and South Americans are also part or pure indigenous Indian and speak one of the many tribal languages.

The southern continent, like the northern, was first inhabited by native peoples. The last great native empires were those of the Aztecs and Mayas in Central America and the Incas in South America. These rich and powerful tribes prospered for centuries. You can still visit their statues, temples, and pyramids in Mexico and Peru.

The emperor of the Incas was said to be descended from the Sun God.

In the 15th century, Spanish and Portuguese explorers crossed the sea in their galleons in search of El Dorado—the fabled golden city—and arrived on the South American Coast. They ruthlessly invaded the native peoples' territories, destroying their great civilizations and stealing their treasures.

Soon after these conquistadores came ships full of European settlers. These new South Americans made their first homes along the Atlantic Coast, then moved farther inland.

The magnificent Iguacu Falls lies on the border between Argentina and Brazil.

From tropical beaches to the windswept tip of Tierra del Fuego

A mixed population

Over centuries, more settlers came from Europe to South America. The population today is made up of four main groups: descendants of European settlers; native South American Indians; *mestizos*, people of both Indian and European blood; and descendants of African slaves brought by Europeans.

Mountains, steamy jungles, sandy beaches

To the west, the rugged Andes Mountains rise through the clouds, crowned with fields of ice and snow. In the center, the Amazon, the biggest river in the world, crosses a huge jungle, the Amazon rainforest. On the other side of the continent, the warm waters of the Caribbean Sea lap sandy beaches on the coast of Venezuela.

To the south are the grassy *pampas,* home to the cattle and the cowboys, called *gauchos,* who herd them. At the tip lie Patagonia and Tierra del Fuego—"the land of fire." In this dry, windswept landscape, no trees grow.

The jagged peaks of the Andes mountain range

The llama lives high in the Andes Mountains.

Along the Venezuelan coast, the water can be crystal clear.

Cape Horn, the barren, southern tip of the continent

Mexico, baked under the hot, tropical sun

Mexico's capital is the second biggest city in the world. Mexico City, one of the world's highest cities, is about 1¼ miles (2 km) above sea level. It was built beside the ruins of the ancient Toltec Indian capital, Teotihuacán, "city of the gods," which flourished 1,400 years ago.

The thousands of factories in Mexico City are the source of much of the city's wealth, pollution, and misery. Many workers come to the city from the countryside and live in shantytowns in desperate poverty.

Mexicans love festivals. There is music everywhere; in the cool evenings, people play guitar and sing of their hopes and dreams. In grand processions, trumpets blare to celebrate the saint who protects each village. On the Day of the Dead, November 1, people visit graves of their friends and relatives. That evening, they dress up like skeletons and dance in the streets.

Mexico is a mixture of Spanish, Indian, and American influences. There are traces of each culture. Deep in the jungle or high in the mountains, temples and palaces of the Mayans and the Aztecs still stand. The Spanish built white churches where Mexicans still worship on Sundays.

Modern banks, shopping malls, and skyscrapers are designed to withstand the earthquakes that often shake Mexico.

Sombreros protect your head from the strong tropical sun. These wide straw hats are only worn by men.

Two Mexican specialties: tortillas and frozen fruit (pineapple, guava, papaya).

Most Mexicans have been Roman Catholics since the conquistadores arrived. The people honor many saints. Some say that the old Aztec gods have even become saints.

The Andes are home to descendants of the Incas.

South of Mexico, Central America is so narrow that the Panama Canal has been dug across it. Boats cross from the Atlantic to the Pacific and back again, without having to sail all the way around the continent. To the south is the continent of South America, made up of 13 countries. Under the peaks of the Andes Mountains, between 9,845 and 16,405 feet (3,000 and 5,000 m), is a land of high plateaus. This is the last home of the Indians who descend from the Incas.

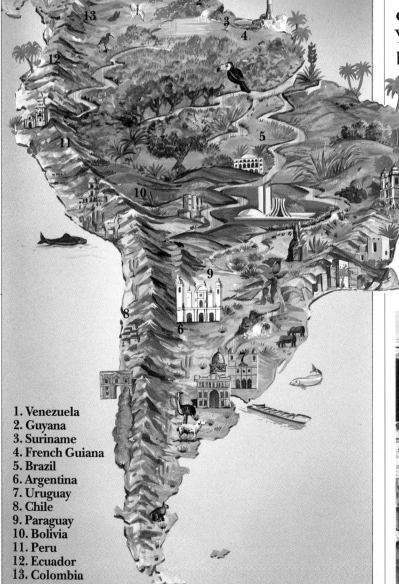

1. Venezuela
2. Guyana
3. Suriname
4. French Guiana
5. Brazil
6. Argentina
7. Uruguay
8. Chile
9. Paraguay
10. Bolivia
11. Peru
12. Ecuador
13. Colombia

In the high Andes, each tribe has its own colorful costumes, traditions, and customs. You can tell to which tribe a woman belongs by the shape of the hat she wears.

Women also wear bright, baggy skirts, one on top of the other, with the oldest ones on the bottom and ponchos, wool shawls that they weave by hand. Meals are often eaten outdoors. The food is spicy, seasoned with hot peppers and coriander. The Mexican diet is based on maize (or corn), potatoes, and tomatoes—three plants that the native people discovered.

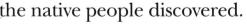

The *capoeira*, a stylized imitation of a fight, is a traditional dance in the region called Bahia.

Brasília, the new capital of Brazil, was built in four years in the middle of a desert.

From Salvador to Rio de Janeiro, from São Paulo to Brasília, the cities of Brazil are all different. Rio de Janeiro is a lively city built around a wide and beautiful bay. Its endless beaches are broken by rocky outcrops that jut out into the ocean like giant teeth. The inhabitants of Rio, who call themselves *Cariocas,* are proud of their city and even more proud of its famous beaches: Ipanema, Copacabana, and Leblon.

Imagine miles of white sand where you can ride your bike, walk, play volleyball, swim, or lounge in the sun.

These candles are *Macumbas*, offerings to the goddess of the sea.

Salvador, farther north along the coast, is a grim reminder of Brazil's history. Here African men, women, and children were unloaded from ships and forced to work as slaves on sugarcane plantations until slavery became illegal in the 19th century. Many Brazilians are descended from African families.

Brazil is a land of many contrasts.

São Paulo, in the south of Brazil, is the country's coffee capital. It has become a thriving business center with traffic and noise, a chaotic jungle of streets and skyscrapers. There is even an airport right in the middle of the city.

The population of São Paulo is increasing so quickly that schools can't be built fast enough. Sometimes two, or even three, classes must share the same room.

Clinging to the hills of Rio are endless *favelas*, **or slum towns.** The thousands of small houses in these ghettoes are just sheets of corrugated iron riveted together. Life is hard for the families here. Some children earn a little money selling ice cream or fruit on the beach.

On the north coast of Brazil, where the white sandy beaches seem to go on forever, the children carry home the fish their fathers have caught. The fishermen go out to sea in twos or threes, standing up on their *jangadas,* which are long boats that look like windsurfing boards. When night falls, they lash themselves to the boat and sleep at sea, out of sight of land. In the morning, the cool breezes carry them back to the beach.

Cuzco, the former Inca capital

Cuzco is in Peru, a high country on the west coast of South America. It is one of the highest cities in the world, perched in the heart of the Andes Mountains. To get there you must catch a train that climbs to more than 16,405 feet (5,000 m), higher than any Rocky Mountain peak. The passengers feel dizzy as they breathe the thin mountain air.

Cuzco was the capital of the Inca empire, which ruled 10 million people. It means "center of the world."

Women come to Cuzco from near and far to sell vegetables and poultry in the market. Others stand on street corners selling mango, banana, or papaya juice to people passing by.

The days are clear and sunny and the nights are very cold. The temperature can drop very quickly when the sun sets.

Farther south, vast plains stretch to the horizon in all directions. These plains are the pampas —like North America's prairies, they are grasslands where huge herds of cattle roam. They are tended by gauchos who work on vast farms, called *haciendas* in Argentina, *fazendas* in Brazil. Gauchos ride great distances over the windy, treeless pampas, watching out for swamps and bogs. The gaucho rides high in the saddle, feet never touching the ground. Like the American cowboy, they catch cattle with a lasso from horseback.

The cowboys of South America, the gauchos, cook their fresh meat over open fires on the pampas.

The stone walls built by the Incas still stand. Though the stones were put together without mortar, they remain secure.

If you were to look down on South America from above the equator, you would see green in all directions. This is the immense Amazon rainforest, an endless jungle fed by the mighty Amazon River.

Here and there, lone houses of the indigenous people stand on stilts over the river. They use boats to go just about everywhere. Even the Incas could not conquer the people who live in the dense jungle.

The Sahara Desert cuts Africa in two.

Hundreds of millions of years ago, the continents were joined together. They were slowly pulled apart, and the Atlantic Ocean poured between them. More recently, one million and 1.9 million years ago, the first humans appeared, before spreading to other continents.

Africans living in the lands north of the Sahara traded with Europeans and shared cultural influences. South of the Sahara, however, the great kingdoms of Mali, Benin, and Zimbabwe remained unknown to the rest of the world until Europeans began to explore the west coast in the 1400s. They finally penetrated the interior in the late 19th century. Most of Africa was controlled by Europeans until the 1950s, but now many African peoples have regained independence.

A village market where nomads sell their animals

The vast Sahara in the north of Africa is the largest desert in the world and is about the size of the United States. In the southeast lies another desert, just as dry and fascinating: the Kalahari. Millions of years ago, the Sahara was green and fertile, but the climate began to change. Less and less rain fell, and the land dried up. Slowly, the desert is spreading across Africa.

Nearer to the equator, it rains more. Grass covers the plains, and thorny trees and bushes give little shade. This is the savanna. Close to the equator, in the heart of Africa, the skies are often cloudy and it rains a lot. Trees and plants love the warm, steamy air, and dense rainforests cover the hills and valleys.

The Tuareg people are always on the move.

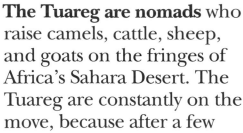

Little boys have their hair shaved off. Teenage boys grow theirs into braids.

The Tuareg are nomads who raise camels, cattle, sheep, and goats on the fringes of Africa's Sahara Desert. The Tuareg are constantly on the move, because after a few weeks in one place, there is nothing left for their animals to eat. The families roll up their tents, collect their belongings, and move on.

In the desert, finding water is everyone's main priority. Each morning, the women trudge several miles to fill their goatskins at the well. Water from the well has to be hauled up by a camel, or by a team of strong men, because the well bucket holds about 11 gallons (40 L) and the well is about 197 feet (60 m) deep.

Traditionally the Tuareg live in tents. Everyone in the camp is related, but each family—usually a husband, wife, and children—lives in a separate tent. About 30 goatskins, tanned and stitched together, are needed to make a tent. The roof is so low a person can't stand up inside. Everyone sleeps on a big platform, except the older boys who sleep out on the ground under the stars.

The goatskin bag is smeared with butter to make it waterproof.

Tuareg children learn Arabic and French at school. Their parents teach them to speak and write in Tuareg, which has its own special alphabet. Instead of using paper, the children write in the desert sand.

The Tuareg wait for their turn at the well.
Shepherds from other camps are there, too,
fetching water for their animals. The well is
a meeting place; people talk and exchange
news with one another.

The Tuareg cook outdoors on camp fires.
Meals are usually millet porridge or
pancakes made from wheat flour, with fresh
or curdled goats' milk. Sometimes a few
dates are added to the meal.

They drink a lot of sweet tea. When people
visit a Tuareg family, they are welcomed with
several glasses of tea.

**In the evening, inside the tent,
women play the *imzad*, which is like a violin.**

**To protect themselves from sun
and wind, the Tuareg wear
loose robes.** These are dyed
blue, and the Tuareg are
called "blue men"
because the color stains their skin. Men
wrap their heads to reveal only their eyes—
they never show their faces to strangers or
important members of their families.
Women don't wear veils, but they sometimes
cover their mouths as a sign of respect.

The villagers work together. They build houses out of clay bricks dried in the sun and thatch the roof with palm leaves. The men cut down trees and clear the undergrowth with machetes to make room for houses and crops. The women plant vegetables like cassava, maize, and yams. There's firewood to collect, washing to be done in the river, and water to be fetched. The women are good at balancing heavy loads on their head. It's a long, hard day under the hot African sun. The men catch fish and hunt monkeys and crocodiles, which make a delicious stew for the evening meal.

People go to the village headman when they need help with their problems and arguments.

What's it like growing up in an African village? Even very young children must learn to help their parents with everyday chores. The girls help crush the cassava roots into a sort of flour called *chikwangue*. They roll the chikwangue into little balls, wrap it in banana leaves, and steam it over an open fire. These dumplings are good for mopping up gravy!

The boys learn how to fish and how to hunt with a bow. Their fathers teach them how to copy the calls of different birds and other animals, to lure them into traps or an arrow's distance.

Women wrap their babies in lengths of cloth and carry them at their hips.

What about school? There isn't a school in every village. Children between the ages of six and 12 often walk for an hour or two each morning to reach the primary school that may be a few miles away. If there is no school building, lessons take place outside, under a tree.

These children are learning French.

Market day is a time to meet friends and talk, as well as to buy and sell. Goods are laid out on pieces of cloth. There are fruits like mangoes, pineapples, papayas, bananas, and coconuts. There are vegetables too, like cassava, sweet potatoes, and chili peppers.

A wedding, the birth of a baby, or a good harvest are all reasons to celebrate. The dancers wear wooden masks and feathered headdresses and paint patterns on their skin. Drums beat out the rhythm and the fun begins! The dancing lasts all night.

Each village has its own special celebration dance with a name like "Dance of Victory" or "Dance of Lightning."

Everyone in this village in the Congo (formerly Zaire) joins in when there's something to celebrate.

There's not much time for playing, but it's fun to kick a ball around or make a car out of wire or wood.

Right in the heart of the Central African rainforests live the Pygmies, an isolated race of people who are trying to keep their ancient way of life. They know every secret of the forest—even which plant makes good toothpaste! Pygmies are not very tall. The men are usually less than five feet (1.5 m) tall. They hunt, fish, and gather fruit and nuts. They are fine musicians and dancers.

The most skillful fishermen are the Wagenia. They drop long reed baskets into the water. If a fish swims into the basket, it gets trapped in the narrow end and can't escape. Sometimes the catch is really big: a catfish can weigh as much as 198 pounds (90 kg)—enough to feed the whole village.

Kinshasa is the capital of Congo, in Central Africa. It stretches across the Congo River, the longest river in Central Africa. Imagine blue sky, hot sun, and the smell of diesel oil and fish. Air-conditioned apartment buildings tower over slums. Streets turn into dirt roads. Bicycle bells jingling, trucks honking, and radios blaring compete with the beat of drums. People greet and visit one another as buses arrive at the water's edge. Canoes jostle around the ships moored at the quay.

People come from the countryside by bus or boat. They come in search of work on building sites or in offices, but many find that there is poverty and hunger in the city too. While they wait to find a better job, they do anything they can to make a little money, such as selling postcards, watermelons, or cigarettes and working odd jobs.

Many parents make long journeys to take their children to school. At the end of the day, the school children, often in uniform, pour into the city streets by the hundreds, talking and laughing.

Asia is the world's most populated continent.

Asia is a land filled with magic. There is mystery and wonder in this great continent that is home to 3.5 billion people, from Turkey to the farthest reaches of China, from Siberia to Borneo.

All the great religions were born here: Judaism, Buddhism, Hinduism, Christianity, and Islam.

Writing was invented in Asia thousands of years ago. So were arithmetic, astronomy, music, cartography, and chemistry.

Camels, antelope, and lions in the Asian savanna

Almost two-thirds of the world's people live in Asia. Some regions are densely populated, whereas others are almost deserted. Great natural barriers like the Himalayan Mountains—the world's highest peaks—and inhospitable deserts, like the Gobi in China, separate and isolate the many different civilizations: Arab, Indian, Chinese, Japanese, and Thai, to name only a few.

To the north lies Siberia, frozen in winter and sweltering in summer. The west and center are dominated by steppes and deserts.

Elephants, herons, macaque monkeys, and wild buffalo live along the river's edge.

In the south, the winds of the monsoon control the rhythm of life. In the winter, they blow toward the sea and keep the land dry. In summer, they blow across the ocean and onto the land, bringing torrential rains that water the rice paddies, turning the fields green.

The jungle in the Bengal Delta is home to cobras, deer, rhinoceroses, storks, crocodiles, monkeys, and tigers.

So many different landscapes, so many different Asians

A Laotian farmer's turban protects him from the sun as he works in rice fields stepped in terraces.

In India, a Mogul emperor had the Taj Mahal built in memory of his wife. It is made of white marble decorated with gemstones.

Long caravans of camels cross Afghanistan to link Iran and Pakistan.

Many of China's great rivers have colors for names. This junk, a traditional boat, is sailing down the Yangtze, or Blue River.

In Vietnam, the farmers work their rice paddies with the help of water buffalo.

Oil is pumped from beneath the desert sands of Arabia. They call it black gold.

Pictured is a Turk in front of St. Sophia in Istanbul. This ancient Christian cathedral was turned into a mosque when Istanbul fell to the Ottoman Turks in 1453.

The Tibetans live in the Himalayan Mountains.

The nomadic Khirgiz people shelter in tents made of yak hides.

The Wailing Wall in Jerusalem, Israel

Russia, shared between Europe and Asia

The colorful domes of St. Basil's church dominate Red Square in Moscow, where the Communist Party ruled from the Kremlin.

Russia is about twice the size of the United States. Until 1991, it was the biggest province in the U.S.S.R., or Soviet Union. The Communist Party ruled the whole country. Now Russia's many neighbors (many former Soviet states) are independent countries such as Estonia, Belarus, the Ukraine, Kazakhstan, and Azerbajan. A quarter of Russia lies in Europe, which ends at the feet of the Ural and Caucasus mountains. The rest of Russia is in Asia: from the steppes to the frozen tundra of Siberia and from the Arctic Ocean to Mongolia. If you caught a train in Moscow, the capital, it would take you seven days and seven nights to reach Vladivostok, on the Sea of Japan!

The immense steppes of Kazakhstan disappear to the horizon in every direction. Only their edges are inhabited.

From icy Siberia to the deserts of Mongolia

The Trans-Siberian Express, the world's longest railroad, crosses Siberia, where the climate is very harsh; it reaches –140° Fahrenheit (–60°C) in winter, and more than 104°F (40°C) in summer.

Most Russians live in Europe, but recently many have moved to Siberia to work in huge mines and oil and gas fields. More than 100 languages are spoken in Russia, but Russian is the most common. The letters are different from the West; Russian uses the Cyrillic alphabet, based on Greek.

Daily life is hard for many Russians. Because of the country's economic problems, even basic essentials are expensive and usually in short supply. In towns, the shops are often empty, and people sometimes have to stand in line for hours to buy staple foods like bread and milk.

In the barren forests and deserts of Mongolia, nomads shelter under traditional tents of heavy canvas.

India: a land of colors and contrasts

India is home to almost one billion people. This peninsula runs from the great Himalayan Mountains to the Indian Ocean. There are many different kinds of terrain: deserts, plains, and jungles. Many Indians live in the countryside, but the cities and towns are overflowing. India has 774 people per square mile (1.3 sq km).

In Rajasthan, the farmers tend goats and camels. The climate is dry. The walls of the houses are a mixture of mud and straw, dried in the hot sun, and roofs are thatched. People sleep on string beds and keep their belongings in painted tin trunks.

In Kerala, a region of rice fields and spice plantations, children go to school by boat. The sea weaves its inlets in and out of the land. People travel by boat along the canals and lagoons, and there are many fishermen.

A village in Rajasthan, in the northwest

A village in Kerala

The wind begins to blow. Clouds rush across the sky. Then rain starts to fall—more and more of it—and the lightning flashes and thunder rumbles.

This is a monsoon, when the rains come and water soaks the ground that has been baked dry by months of sunshine. Life is reborn in the monsoon rains. Palm trees buckle in the wind, and rice fields  are flooded. The great rivers of India, the Ganges, Indus, Krishna, and Brahmanputra, burst their banks and flood the nearby land. Though many fields are now irrigated, the monsoon is still important. Without it the farmers would have little to harvest, and they would go hungry. But if the monsoon is too violent, then the crops are damaged and there will not be enough to eat.

After the monsoon has passed, winter sets in. In the north, the nights are cold, and people wrap up well to keep warm. In the south, winters are mild.

Summer starts around the end of March. By May it is so hot that the tar melts on the streets. In the houses, big fans help cool the air. At night, people sleep outside.

Indians eat with the fingers of their right hand. Meals are usually eaten with rice, or with cakes of wheat or millet called *chapattis,* which are used to pick up the vegetables or meat. There are many different curries, spicy stews of meat, fish, or vegetables.

Women wear a *sari*. This is a brightly colored piece of silk or cotton cloth 18 feet (5.5 m) long, which is wrapped around the waist and draped over the left shoulder. The men wear a *kurta,* a collarless shirt, over tight cotton trousers called *churidar,* or over a length of cloth wrapped round the waist and tucked between the legs called a *dhoti.*

The bridegroom may arrive at his fiancée's house on a beautifully dressed horse, accompanied by a younger brother or sister.

A marriage is an important event in Indian society. Parents are involved in choosing a partner for their son or daughter. When the groom lifts up the bride's veil, it may be the first time he has ever seen her. In Rajasthan, the ceremony takes place at night at the bride's house.

The bride's hands and feet are decorated with fine patterns traced in a vegetable dye called henna.

Weddings are splendid and cost a lot of money. The bride and groom, dressed in the finest silk and brocade, walk seven times around a holy fire. The couple live in the groom's house, where the groom's mother rules the household.

The Ganges is a sacred river for all Hindus.

In the Hindu religion, God has millions of different forms. The three main forms are *Brahma, Vishnu,* and *Shiva*. Children learn about them by hearing stories from the *Ramayana* and the *Mahabharata,* sacred tales about the gods and their battles. All Hindus revere the Ganges River; Hinduism began on its banks. Hindus believe that if you bathe in the river water, your sins will be washed away.

India is a land of festivals. There are many feasts to celebrate holidays and honor gods. Some feasts last for several days. *Diwali* is the festival of light. In the north they celebrate Diwali at the beginning of the new year. Each house glimmers with the light of thousands of tiny oil lamps, and children set off fireworks.

The festival of *Holi* is celebrated with flags and drums.

Hindus believe that after someone dies, the soul is born again as some other living thing: a person, animal, or insect. This is called reincarnation. They believe that if you die in Varanasi, a holy city on the banks of Ganges, you will not have to be reincarnated again; you will be in paradise.

Japan: "Land of the Rising Sun"

According to Japanese tradition, "where the sun bursts forth from the sea, there is Japan." The Japanese are also known as Nippons. In their language that means "they who make the sun rise." A bright red sun is the symbol of the country and appears on the flag. Japan is in the Pacific Ocean. When it's bedtime in the U.S., it's lunchtime in Japan.

From north to south there are almost 3,000 islands in the Japanese archipelago. The names of the four largest are snowy Hokkaido in the north; Honshu, home to Mount Fuji and the capital Tokyo; and Kyushu and Shikoku, to the south.

Japanese floors are covered with mats of woven cane. To keep them clean, people take off their shoes before going indoors.

Earthquakes happen regularly in Japan. Most of the time, they are little tremors that people can't even feel. But in the past, some horrible earthquakes have rocked Japan. The huge 1923 quake flattened most of Tokyo. Now houses are made of wood and raised on pylons to stand up to the shaking.

Tall buildings are also earthquake-proof, with special pylons that will sway—but not fall over—if the earth begins to move.

Everything in a Japanese house is light and easy to move. The windows don't have glass, and the inner walls are sliding screens made of squares of delicate rice paper.

Sushi is raw fish.

Fish is always on the menu in Japan. The Japanese catch more fish than any other nation and eat much more of it than Westerners do. They often eat sushi, raw fish cut in cubes and dipped in a spicy sauce. They also enjoy seaweed, served as a vegetable or in soups.

The Japanese sit on a cushion on their knees at a low table and use chopsticks to pick up the cubes of food.

A festival kimono

Beds unroll and roll up again. A futon, a cozy quilt with a mattress, is tucked away in a cupboard during the day. At night it is stretched out on the matted floor.

Futons save space and are comfortable.

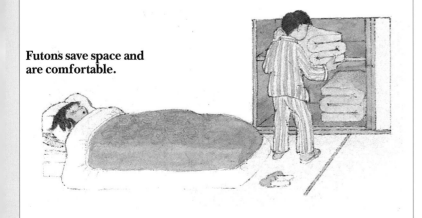

Japanese baths follow an ancient tradition. The water is very hot, and the whole family bathes together. Whether they are at home or in the public bath, everyone soaps up and rinses off before they go into the tub or pool, so the shared water stays clean for the others. The bathers climb out shiny, red, and very relaxed.

Two ways to tie an *obi*, the wide belt that holds a kimono (robe) in place.

Crowds rush and push through the busy streets of Tokyo.

During rush hour when people are going to or from work, pushers squeeze commuters into trains and force the doors closed.

Tokyo, with its endless suburbs, is one of Asia's busiest cities. Crowds dash through the streets to work. In Tokyo, the streets have no proper names, and buildings have no real numbers. But somehow letters are delivered anyway!

Paintbrush and ink

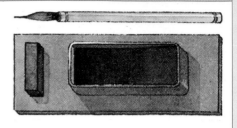

How do you write in Japanese? Not with the 26 letters of our alphabet, but with little drawings called characters. Each represents a word or an idea. There are several hundred thousand all together. To read well, people need to learn 2,000 characters. Children just learning the language start with 46 symbols.

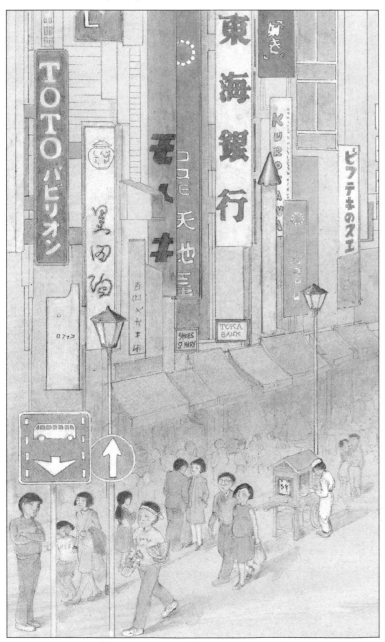

Great competitions between kites take place every year. Kite festivals occur all over Asia. The kites are huge and beautifully decorated. It takes a whole team on the ground to maneuver a single kite. Each team tries to sever the lines of their opponents' kite. Thin strings that hold up the kite can cut someone's hands like glass.

On the kite below you can see the symbol of Japan, the red sun.

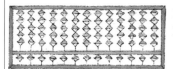

In the era of the calculator, many people still count with an abacus.

Japan has two main religions: Shintoism, born in Japan, and Buddhism, which came from India. Shintoists worship many gods. The Shinto procession below is moving toward a temple. Drums and cymbals guide the steps of the priests, who are carrying a statue of a god. Buddhists follow the teaching of an Indian monk who was given the name of Buddha, or "Enlightened One."

More people live in China than in any other country in the world. There are more than 1.2 billion people in China. More than 5.7 million live in Beijing, the capital. From six o'clock in the morning, crowds fill the streets. Peddlers are everywhere selling their goods and services—one offers to repair your bike, another to clean your ears. Tiananmen Square, in the heart of the city, is the largest public open space in the world.

China is a great power. It is also a poor country. Every year the number of people increases by about 12 million. Only 15 percent of China's land can produce food, so trying to feed everyone is a problem. This is why the government encourages couples to have only one child. Today, a Chinese child may be an only child, with no brothers or sisters.

Until 1985 children were not required to go to school. Many Chinese people cannot read or write. Many families living in the country think it is more important for children to work in the fields, helping to bring in food for the family.

The Chinese love birds and will often go for walks carrying caged birds with them.

How do people get around in China? Most people travel by bicycle. People from the country use carts pulled by donkeys to take their fruit and vegetables to market. The buses are always packed full of people, and they move very slowly through the crowds of cyclists and pedestrians.

Chinese, but also Tibetan, Mongol, and Manchu

The Dalai Lama, the living god of the Tibetans, used to live in Potala, on the roof of the world, 22,966 feet (7,000 m) above sea level.

The Huang River (3,100 miles [5,000 km] long) floods often and is called the Scourge of China. The Yangtze (3,596 miles [5,800 km] long) is safer.

From the high plateaus of Tibet to deserts and forests of bamboo, there is every imaginable kind of landscape in China. And not everyone who lives there is Chinese. Tibetans, Manchus, and Mongols live there too, but the Chinese outnumber them all. These other groups are ethnic minorities.

The giant panda is the national symbol of China. Giant pandas live in bamboo forests, and they eat just one type of bamboo. There are not many giant pandas left. These huge black and white animals are extremely strong and have long, razor-sharp claws.

The Great Wall of China is so huge that it can be seen from the Moon! Building work was started on the wall about 200 B.C. by the Qin Emperor Shi Huangdi, who wanted to keep out hostile invaders coming in from the north.

In the tropical south of China, where palm trees and bamboo thickets grow, water buffalo help farmers till the rice fields.

The oasis of Turpan, in the middle of the northeastern deserts, is famous for its beautiful Muslim mosque.

In southern China, farmers grow rice on terraces and harvest it two or three times a year.

The nomads of Mongolia herd their horses and put up their *yurts*, tents of skin or felt, out on the frozen plain.

A teahouse in Shanghai

Tea is the national drink of China. It was discovered by a Chinese emperor. The usual tea is green tea, bought in small packets. The Chinese drink tea at any hour of the day and night. They also like hot water. A thermos of boiled water is kept on hand for drinking and making tea.

In the south, most people eat rice at every meal. In north China, they prefer bread rolls or noodles made with eggs and flour. When Marco Polo visited China in the 13th century, he discovered these noodles and took some back to Italy with him. The Italians liked them so much that pasta soon became their national dish.

The Chinese do not use butter or cheese, and all the fresh milk is saved for the children. Grownups drink soy milk, which is made from soybeans. They often finish a meal with soup.

Suzhou, with its hundreds of canals, is called the Venice of China. It stands on the Grand Canal, which joins the Yangtze River to Beijing.

Chinese dishes: noodles, hundred-year eggs, shark fins, black mushrooms, roast duck, steamed buns, and ginger

Most Chinese live in the countryside.

An outdoor restaurant in Beijing: in the evening, parks and pavements are crowded with people taking a walk, talking to friends, and playing board games. It is difficult to be alone in China.

Eight out of every 10 Chinese people live in the country. Many people work in the paddy fields in their bare feet, up to their ankles in water. Children help their parents to tend pigs or ducks.

Islands in the ocean: Australasia

On the opposite side of the world from New York and London is Australasia, which includes Australia, New Zealand, and the thousands of islands of Polynesia. Australia is a huge island nearly as big as the U.S. In many ways, Australia is our opposite. Daytime in North America is nighttime in Australia. Our spring is their fall.

The Aborigines were the first people to live in Australia. They came across the sea in prehistoric times, probably from southeast Asia. The first European settlers were British convicts sentenced to exile in Australia in 1788. When gold was discovered in 1851, settlers came from all over the world and seized the Aborigines' sacred homelands.

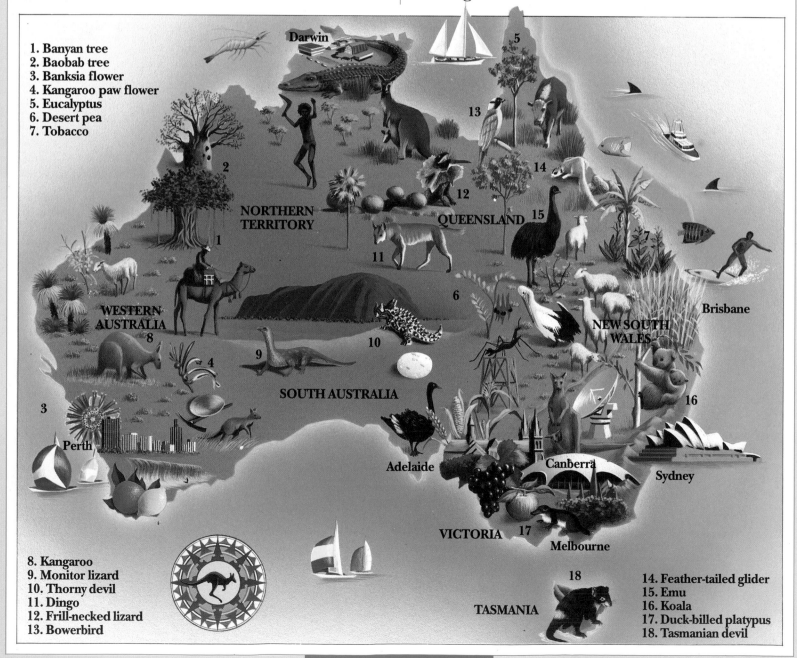

1. Banyan tree
2. Baobab tree
3. Banksia flower
4. Kangaroo paw flower
5. Eucalyptus
6. Desert pea
7. Tobacco

8. Kangaroo
9. Monitor lizard
10. Thorny devil
11. Dingo
12. Frill-necked lizard
13. Bowerbird

14. Feather-tailed glider
15. Emu
16. Koala
17. Duck-billed platypus
18. Tasmanian devil

Darwin

NORTHERN TERRITORY

QUEENSLAND

WESTERN AUSTRALIA

SOUTH AUSTRALIA

NEW SOUTH WALES

Brisbane

Perth

Adelaide

Canberra

Sydney

VICTORIA

Melbourne

TASMANIA

Australia is the land of kangaroos, koalas, and kookaburras.

The pioneers who settled Australia's outback had to clear trees, build houses and boats, and make roads. Then the farmers started to plant crops and establish huge herds of sheep and cattle.

The bird of paradise, a visitor from New Guinea

Weird and wondrous desert dwellers

It looks fierce, but the thorny devil, a little dragon lizard, is no bigger than your hand and only eats ants. This blue-tongued lizard is about 18 inches (45 cm) long. Surprise it when it's basking in the sun, and it may hiss and stick out its tongue—but it's harmless.

Listen! The loud cackle of laughter overhead is the kookaburra: "Merry, merry king of the bush is he." What sounds like a tinkling bell is the bellbird; a soft low whistle followed by the sound of a sharp crack of a whip is the whipbird. The emu, one of the tallest birds in the world, lives here too. It can't fly, but it can run very, very fast!

The wombat lives in a burrow like a badger. This plump, furry marsupial has strong paws and shovel-like claws for digging.

In the dead of night an eerie howl shatters the silence, echoed by an answering howl farther off. Dingoes are calling to each other. These wild dogs roam the land in small packs like wolves, hunting rabbits and other animals.

Kangaroos are the most famous of all Australia's marsupials. When a baby kangaroo, or "joey," is born, it crawls straight into its mother's pouch. After awhile it will venture out to eat grass, diving back into the pouch headfirst when frightened. Marsupials are animals that carry their babies in a pouch for the first months of their lives. These animals come in all shapes and sizes, from wallabies and koalas to tiny marsupial mice that hop like kangaroos.

An outdoor life—in the city
Australian cities are like any others: busy, noisy, and filled with traffic. But because their weather is often warm and dry, Australian children spend a lot of time outdoors. Schoolchildren eat packed lunches outside throughout the year. Even in mid-winter they can have a barbecue or a birthday party in the park, among the joggers and sunbathers.

Beyond the high buildings, you can catch sight of the deep blue ocean glittering in the sun.

On surfboards or in long rowboats, lifesavers rescue swimmers caught in the surf.

Beaches stretch as far as the eye can see.
Australia has more beaches than any other country in the world. The sea never gets very cold, so people sail, swim, and surf all year round—they also go deep-sea diving, windsurfing, and fishing. Australian children are good swimmers, but they are taught to stay close to shore. There may be dangerous currents or even sharks farther out.

The Australian bush begins where the city ends.
Bushwalking is a serious business, and people must be prepared with tough shoes or boots, a hat, a backpack, water, a good map, and a "billy can" for brewing tea.

The flying doctor pays a call. Stations have airstrips where small planes can land.

Can you imagine living so far out in the country that your nearest neighbors are several hours' drive away?

That is the Australian outback, dry and endless. Farmers and their families live on huge stations, often hundreds of miles apart.

The roads are just dirt. The "jackaroos," or farm workers, used to round up the huge herds of sheep on horseback. But now they use motorcycles, trucks, and even helicopters for these round-ups.

What about school? Some children don't go to school—school comes to them, by radio. They do their work by tuning in to the "School of the Air."

The teachers may be many hundreds of miles away, but the pupils can talk to their teachers as if they were together in one big classroom.

The farmhouse is designed to keep out the heat and the flies. Many houses stand on stilts, so that snakes can't get in. There are screens on the doors and windows. Rainwater runs off of the corrugated iron roof and is collected in rain tanks. Children soon learn to help around the station with different chores. Most of them have horses of their own and are good riders.

NEXT 10 km

Kangaroos crossing!

Perhaps you have seen pictures of tropical islands —wonderful places with palm trees and soft sand, surrounded by warm, clear seas. The islands are like gardens, full of flowers and delicious fruit. Under the sea, fish swim among beautiful shells, plants, and coral.

The tropics lie in the orange and red bands on the map, near the equator.

An island called Nossy-Be is a typical tropical island. It lies northwest of Madagascar, off the coast of Africa. In the Malagasy language, "Nossy-Be" means "big island."

There are many other tropical islands, such as Hawaii, Tahiti, the West Indies, and the Galapagos Islands. They are all near the Equator, between the tropic of Cancer to the north and the tropic of Capricorn to the south.

People build their houses above the ground on little stilts, so water cannot get into them during stormy weather.

Shark: best avoided so you don't end up as its meal!

The waters around the tropical island Nossy-Be are filled with a great variety of delicious fish. And nearly everyone on these islands lives by fishing.

Fishermen can make their own canoe out of a hardwood tree. They use a small ax to hollow out the tree. To make the canoe stable, they fit it with a frame called an outrigger, which balances the canoe as it floats. The sail is a square of cotton.

On feast days, the young men race each other. The whole village lines up on the beach to watch.

Grouper

Ray

Going fishing

As soon as the sun is up, fishermen lay baskets on the sea bottom. By nightfall they will be full of small fish. Next they drop a net from the back of their canoes as they paddle toward the shore. When they draw in the net, it becomes crammed with exotic fish with strange-sounding names: threadfin, barracuda, tiger fish, and parrot fish. In no time, the fish will all be eaten, grilled or raw, soaked in coconut milk.

The easiest place to fish is in a lagoon, separated from the open sea by a wall of brilliant coral. The calm water here is the color of turquoise.

Barracuda

The fishermen attach the fish to poles and carry them to the houses.

Bananas, coconuts, and sugarcane thrive in the tropical sunshine.

Each family builds its own house. The walls are made of bamboo canes and banana leaves. The roof is covered with coconut palms.

At the market: cinnamon sticks, mild and hot chilies, pineapples, and many kinds of bananas.

In the middle of the island, farmers grow sugarcane in huge fields.

Spices for flavoring food

Cooking is usually done outside. Fish is cooked over open fires, and there are lots of vegetables, salads, and rice. Maniocs and yams grow underground like potatoes. The leaves of maniocs can also be eaten. Turmeric, another root vegetable, has a strong taste. It is powdered and used for flavoring food.

Sugar and spice and everything nice

Spices are flavorful. Just a little can give food a new taste. The hottest spices are red and green chilies. If you're not used to them, they make your mouth feel like it's on fire!

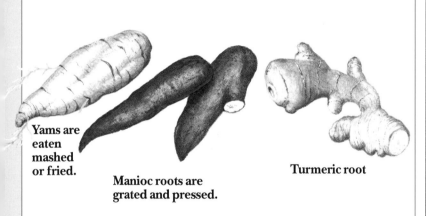

Yams are eaten mashed or fried.

Manioc roots are grated and pressed.

Turmeric root

Vanilla is a precious spice. The plant has a beautiful yellow flower. The fruit hangs in bunches of green pods, which grow dark and sweet-smelling as they dry. Vanilla ice cream gets its flavor from these pods.

Every part of a coconut is useful. The clear "milk" is like fresh water; the white flesh can be eaten by itself or used for making cakes, oil, candles, and even soap; and coconut oil is good for your skin. The hairy outside part of the coconut is used to make mats, and the hard shells make good bowls. Children climb palm trees to pick the coconuts that grow on them.

Zebus are cow-like animals with a hump that stores fat.

Every winter cyclones sweep across the tropical island. Violent winds whip up waves higher than houses. Crops can be flattened, trees uprooted, and houses swept away. After two or three days, the sun comes out again.

Greenland: a land of ice in the far north, home to the Inuit

Greenland, the largest island in the world, is in the Arctic Circle. The people who live here were first called Eskimos by their neighbors, the Algonquin Indians, and then by explorers. They call themselves "Inuit," which means "the real people." They live on the snowy shores of the island; farther inland, it is a huge ice cap. In winter the sun barely rises over the horizon. In some places, the sun does not rise for months.

Inuit boy

Inuits developed excellent hunting and fishing skills, because it is too cold to grow any fruit or vegetables in the frozen ground. The villages are small, because few people live in these cold places. The gaily painted houses brighten up the white landscape. Today, almost all the villages have electricity and other modern conveniences. The Inuits still hunt seals and polar bears, though. The skins are dried and kept outside in the icy air.

There are almost twice as many dogs as there are people in Greenland.

Traditional outdoor dress includes two pairs of boots, pants made of bear skin, and an *anorak*, or heavy coat, made of sealskin or caribou hide. Dressed like this, people can go out even when the temperature is −120° Fahrenheit (−50°C).

The winter evenings are long and dark.

Kayaks and sleds are laid across frames so that the dogs won't chew the leather.

In the heat near the stove, which served for both heating and cooking, women traditionally tanned hides while the men made harpoons and the children played games. They ate meat or fish, either dried or boiled; seal blubber; and rice. Their water came from melted ice. In early times the people covered the walls of their huts with sealskins to keep in the warmth. Not so long ago they were covered with newspapers. Now, many Inuit houses are built with modern materials.

A woman chews a piece of seal leather to make it soft to sew.

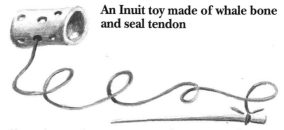
An Inuit toy made of whale bone and seal tendon

Inuits live in other countries too. Some make their home in northern Canada, Alaska, or Siberia, in the far north of Russia. They don't all speak the same native language, but they have much in common and can usually understand each other.

A shop in Greenland sells tools and supplies.

A driver needs as many as 15 dogs to pull a sled. The lead dog is often a female; the other dogs may be her grown-up puppies.

An Inuit seal hunter hides behind a white screen held up by small skis. Only his gun pokes through as he creeps up on the seal.

Seals were a precious part of the traditional Inuit lifestyle. They provided meat, blubber, oil, skins, bones for toys and tools, and tendons for thread.

Hunting by kayak: the kayak is a long, thin canoe made of sealskins stretched over a wooden frame. There is room for one person.

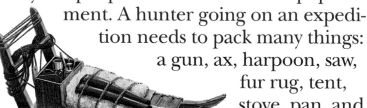

Dogs are still used to pull the Inuits' sleds on hunting or fishing expeditions, although today the people also use modern equipment. A hunter going on an expedition needs to pack many things: a gun, ax, harpoon, saw, fur rug, tent, stove, pan, and plenty of food. All this is tied to the sled with seal-tendon rope. A team of dogs pulls the sled, with the most intelligent dog in front as leader. The dogs are strong and can pull heavy loads. The master gives his orders to the leader. To make the dogs turn right, their master shouts "illi-illi," to make them go left, "ka-ka." Going downhill, the dogs are tied behind the sled to make it slow down.

The dogs sleep outside. Their thick fur protects them from the cold as they lie curled up in the snow, their noses tucked under their tails. When they get up, they crack their way out of a shell of snow.

In shark fishing, the fisherman makes a hole in the ice and drops a line. When the shark takes the bait, the fisherman harpoons the shark and pulls it out of the water, where it freezes right away in the cold air.

How do you make an igloo?

Inside an igloo, seen from above

Bone knife
Snow saw

Inside an igloo, from the side

When the hunters have cut the blocks, they pile them like bricks one on top of the other, in a spiral shape like a snail's shell. The hardened blocks form an icy shelter that keeps out the cold wind. Light passes through the ice, so the inside of the igloo is bright and cheerful. The hunters cut benches out of the hard snow to sit on. Then they light a fire and heat up some soup for dinner inside their ice home! The fire's smoke and fumes escape through a small hole in the roof.

When Inuit hunters are too far from their village to return in the evening, they build a snow house: an igloo. They cut out big blocks of hard snow with a saw. In earlier times, they used a bone knife.

Shark meat, when prepared the right way, can be good to eat.

All around the world . . .

Following the name of each country is its capital.

EUROPE
1. Albania, Tiranë
2. Austria, Vienna
3. Belgium, Brussels
4. Bulgaria, Sofia
5. Denmark, Copenhagen
6. Greenland, Nuuk (Gothab)
7. Finland, Helsinki
8. France, Paris
9. Germany, Berlin
10. Greece, Athens
11. Hungary, Budapest
12. Iceland, Reykjavik
13. Ireland, Dublin
14. Italy, Rome
15. Netherlands, Amsterdam
16. Norway, Oslo
17. Poland, Warsaw
18. Portugal, Lisbon
19. Romania, Bucharest
20. Spain, Madrid
21. Sweden, Stockholm
22. Switzerland, Bern
23. United Kingdom of Great Britain, London
    Bermuda
    England
    Falkland Islands
    Gibraltar
    Northern Ireland
    South Sandwich Islands
    Scotland
    Wales
24. Yugoslavia, Belgrade

AMERICAS
25. Argentina, Buenos Aires
26. Belize, Belmopan
27. Bolivia, La Paz
28. Brazil, Brasília
29. Canada, Ottawa
30. Chile, Santiago
31. Colombia, Bogotá
32. Costa Rica, San José
33. Cuba, Havana
34. Dominican Republic, Santo Domingo
35. Ecuador, Quito
36. El Salvador, San Salvador
37. French Guiana, Cayenne
38. Guatemala, Guatemala City
39. Guyana, Georgetown
40. Haiti, Port-au-Prince
41. Honduras, Tegucigalpa
42. Jamaica, Kingston
43. Mexico, Mexico City
44. Nicaragua, Managua
45. Panama, Panama
46. Paraguay, Asunción
47. Peru, Lima
48. Suriname, Paramaribo
49. United States of America, Washington, D.C.
50. Uruguay, Montevideo
51. Venezuela, Caracas

AFRICA
52. Algeria, Algiers
53. Angola, Luanda
54. Benin, Porto-Novo
55. Botswana, Gaborone
56. Burkina Faso, Ouagadoughou
57. Burundi, Bujumbura
58. Cameroon, Yaoundé
59. Central African Republic, Bangui
60. Chad, Ndjemena
61. Congo, Kinshasa
62. Congo Republic, Brazzaville
63. Egypt, Cairo
64. Equatorial Guinea, Malabo
65. Ethiopia, Addis Ababa
66. Gabon, Libreville
67. Gambia, Banjul
68. Ghana, Accra
69. Guinea, Conakry
70. Guinea-Bissau, Bissau
71. Ivory Coast, Yamoussoukro
72. Kenya, Nairobi
73. Lesotho, Maseru
74. Liberia, Monrovia
75. Libya, Tripoli
76. Madagascar, Antananarivo
77. Malawi, Lilongwe
78. Mali, Bamako
79. Mauritania, Nouakchott
80. Morocco, Rabat
81. Mozambique, Maputo
82. Namibia, Windhoek
83. Niger, Niamey
84. Nigeria, Abuja
85. Rwanda, Kigali
86. Senegal, Dakar
87. Sierra Leone, Freetown
88. Somalia, Mogadishu
89. South Africa, Pretoria
90. Sudan, Khartoum
91. Swaziland, Mbabane
92. Tanzania, Dodoma
93. Togo, Lomé
94. Tunisia, Tunis
95. Uganda, Kampala
96. Zambia, Lusaka
97. Zimbabwe, Harare

ASIA
98. Afghanistan, Kabul
99. Bangladesh, Dhaka
100. Bhutan, Thimbu
101. Brunei, Bandar Seri Begawan
102. Cambodia, Phnom Penh
103. China, Beijing
     Hong Kong
104. India, New Delhi
105. Indonesia, Jakarta
106. Iran, Tehran
107. Iraq, Baghdad
108. Israel, Jerusalem
109. Japan, Tokyo
110. Jordan, Amman
111. Kuwait, Kuwait City
112. Laos, Vientiane
113. Malaysia, Kuala Lumpur
114. Mongolia, Ulan Bator
115. Myanmar, Yangôn
116. Nepal, Kathmandu
117. North Korea, Pyongyang
118. Oman, Muscat
119. Pakistan, Islamabad
120. Philippines, Manila
121. Qatar, Doha
122. Saudi Arabia, Riyadh
123. Singapore, Singapore
124. Sri Lanka, Colombo
125. South Korea, Seoul
126. Syria, Damascus
127. Taiwan, Taipei
128. Thailand, Bangkok
129. Turkey, Ankara
130. United Arab Emirates, Abu Dhabi
131. Vietnam, Hanoi
132. Yemen, Sana

AUSTRALASIA
133. Australia, Canberra
134. New Zealand, Wellington
135. Papua New Guinea, Port Moresby

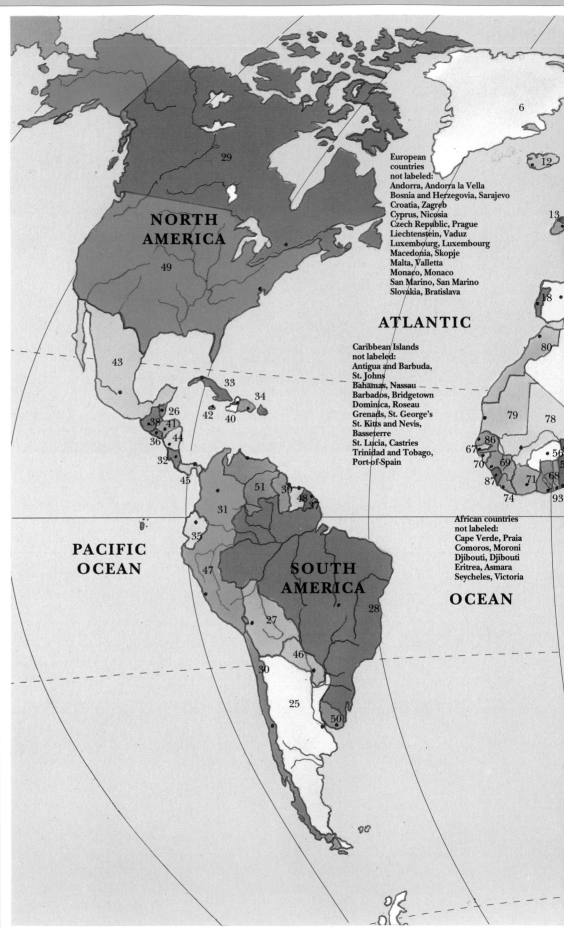

NORTH AMERICA

ATLANTIC

European countries not labeled:
Andorra, Andorra la Vella
Bosnia and Herzegovia, Sarajevo
Croatia, Zagreb
Cyprus, Nicosia
Czech Republic, Prague
Liechtenstein, Vaduz
Luxembourg, Luxembourg
Macedonia, Skopje
Malta, Valletta
Monaco, Monaco
San Marino, San Marino
Slovakia, Bratislava

Caribbean Islands not labeled:
Antigua and Barbuda, St. Johns
Bahamas, Nassau
Barbados, Bridgetown
Dominica, Roseau
Grenads, St. George's
St. Kitts and Nevis, Basseterre
St. Lucia, Castries
Trinidad and Tobago, Port-of-Spain

African countries not labeled:
Cape Verde, Praia
Comoros, Moroni
Djibouti, Djibouti
Eritrea, Asmara
Seycheles, Victoria

PACIFIC OCEAN

SOUTH AMERICA

OCEAN

ARCTIC
OCEAN

Former Soviet States
not labeled:
Armenia, Yerevan
Azerbaijan, Baku
Belarus, Minsk
Estonia, Tallinn
Kazakhstan, Almaty
Kyrgystan, Bishkek

Latvia, Riga
Lithuania, Vilnius
Moldava, Chisinau
Russian Federation, Moscow
Slovenia, Ljubljana
Tajikistan, Dushanbe
Turkmenistan, Ashghabat
Ukraine, Kiev

ASIA

EUROPE

AFRICA

PACIFIC
OCEAN

Pacific Islands not labeled:
Fiji, Suva
Kiribati, Tarawa
Marshall Islands, Majuro
Micronesia, Palikir
Nauru, Yaren
Palau, Koror
Samoa, Apia
Solomon Islands, Honiara
Tonga, Nuku'alofa
Tuvalu, Funafuti Atoll
Vannatu, Port Vila

Asia not labeled:
Bahrain, Manama
Lebanon, Beirut

INDIAN
OCEAN

Indian Ocean islands not labeled:
Maldives, Male
Mauritius, Port Louis

AUSTRALASIA

Intriguing facts, activities, games, a quiz, and a glossary, followed by the index

■ Did you know?

There are many different written languages. Thousands of years ago, the ancient Egyptians wrote in hieroglyphics. In 1824, Jean-Francois Champollion of France deciphered them. Some hieroglyphs are simple pictures—a plant, an animal, or an object—a form of pictograms. The Chinese and Japanese write with pictograms, and many characters have the same meaning in both languages.

The Aborigines, the first inhabitants of Australia, use four colors in their bark paintings: red and yellow, which are both made from ocher in the ground, white from chalk, and black from charcoal.

Egyptian scribes—full-time writers—painted hieroglyphs on fine rolls of papyrus, a plant that still grows on the banks of the Nile River in Egypt.

The "Milky Way Dreaming" is a story the Aborigines often painted. Dreamtime stories tell how the universe was made.

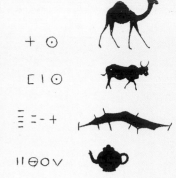

The Tuareg people of the Sahara Desert have their own language, *Tifinagh,* with its own special alphabet. Children learn to read and write by drawing characters and forming sentences in the sand. Above is how you write "camel," "tent," "cow," and "teapot" in Tifinagh.

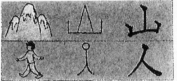

Draw four pictograms! Japanese = English = Chinese

ki = tree = *mú*
té = hand = *shŏu*
yama = mountain = *shān*
hito = man = *rén*

These four characters are all pictograms. To draw them, you will need a long paintbrush that you dip in Chinese ink. Writing isn't just a way of communicating—it's also an art called calligraphy.

How do you climb onto a camel? First you have to persuade it to get down on its knees—and that might take a long time! A camel moves its legs in pairs as it sways along, first the left ones, then the right. Riding on its back is like sitting in a boat on a rough sea!

Camels tramp endlessly across the desert. Their large feet prevent them from sinking into the sand. They can carry a load of 331 pounds (150 kg), walk 31 miles (50 km) in one day, and go for days without water. At the end of a journey, the camel drinks a lot of water.

Camels are useful in many other ways too. Females provide milk, which is turned into cheese and yogurt. Camel dung is burned as fuel.

How do Pygmies live? Pygmies were the first inhabitants of central Africa. They live in the heart of the rainforest near the equator. Few Pygmies are more than five feet (1.5 m) tall.

They know every plant in the forest; their houses are made from looped branches covered with overlapping leaves, and even their soap and toothpaste are made from plants. Pygmies are famous for their medical skills. Music and dance are also important in Pygmy culture.

In India, many women put on colorful makeup and glittering jewelry.

If a woman wears red powder in the part of her hair, it lets others know she is married.

Some women also decorate their foreheads with a dot of red paint, a *tika*. Village women wear heavy silver jewelry both day and night.

Women in Rajasthan, in northwest India, wear these types of jewels. In town, women prefer rings and bracelets of fine gold.

■ Do you know the martial arts?

Samurai (Japanese warriors from the Middle Ages) knew many secret ways of fighting. Today these ways are known as the martial arts.

The martial arts are not just practiced in Japan—they are popular in most countries and are even part of the Olympics.

Kyodo is the Japanese art of archery. Archers need great concentration to hold the bow, stretch the bowstring, and aim at the target.

Kendo **is like fencing. The sword of long ago has been replaced with a long bamboo rod.**

Sumo is part sport, part show business. The Japanese love to watch sumo! It is a battle between two enormous wrestlers—331 pounds (150 kg) of bulging muscle and fat. The aim of the game is to get a grip on your opponent and push him out of the circle painted on the floor. The struggle only lasts a few seconds. The great sumo wrestlers are popular stars with many adoring fans.

Judo and *judokas*

There are no weapons in judo, just handholds and violent kicks.

Before the struggle begins, the *judokas* bow to one another with great ceremony.

The colors of their belts show the level that each person has reached. Beginners wear white or yellow belts, and champions wear blue or, the ultimate, black belts.

The aim is to knock over your opponent and pin him or her to the ground. Doing this takes control and concentration.

Karate is an art practiced without weapons, like judo. It involves powerful blows of the hand.

■ Quiz

Can you answer these questions? The correct answers are at the bottom of the page.

1. What symbol appears on Japan's flag?
a. a yellow fish
b. a red sun
c. a blue cross

2. What continent is the smallest in the world?
a. Australia
b. Asia
c. Africa

3. How long is winter in Norway and Finland?
a. one or two months
b. seven or eight months
c. six weeks

4. Japan is made up of
a. 10,000 islands.
b. 500 islands.
c. 3,000 islands.

5. France's Bastille Day commemorates
a. the French Revolution.
b. the president's birthday
c. the first day of spring

6. Canada's two official languages are English and
a. Spanish.
b. French.
c. Latin.

7. Tierra del Fuego is the southern most tip of
a. Asia.
b. South America.
c. Africa.

8. A lagoon is separated from the open sea by a wall of
a. shells.
b. coral.
c. seaweed.

9. The largest island in the world (not a continent) is
a. Hawaii.
b. Hokkaido.
c. Greenland.

10. In China's cities, how do most people get around?
a. They ride in cars.
b. They ride motor scooters.
c. They ride bicycles

11. The national symbol of China is
a. calligraphy.
b. the giant panda.
c. a kite.

12. Centuries ago, the Incas lived in
a. Mexico.
b. the Andes mountains.
c. the African Sahara.

13. The European Union (E.U.) includes
a. seven countries.
b. 12 countries.
c. all the countries of Europe.

14. Canada's capital is
a. Vancouver.
b. Ottawa.
c. Moose Jaw.

■ Games and activities

Do you know how to throw a boomerang?
Getting it to come back is not easy!

Always throw a boomerang downward as if you were aiming at the ground a few feet in front of you. Raise your arm and let the boomerang go as your arm comes down. It should loop around and up. But getting it right takes practice! Be careful not to throw a boomerang near houses or people—it is a dangerous weapon.

A collection of seashells from the Indian Ocean
There are hundreds of kinds of shells on the island of Nossy-Be. Children collect them in the lagoons and on the beach. After a swim, children lie in the shade of coconut palms, making necklaces out of shells or using shells as counters in their games. At low tide you might even find the shell of a giant clam. When the clams are under the sea, their lips are a phosphorescent blue!

1, 2, and 3 are cones
4 and 12 are murex
5, 10, and 11 are clams
6, 7, 8, and 9 are cowries

Giant clam

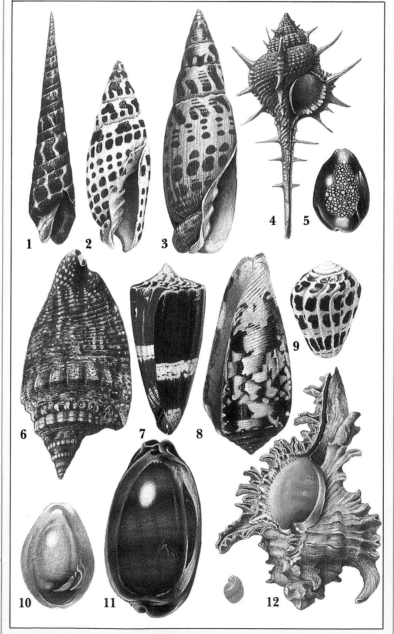

1 2 3 4 5

6 7 8 9

10 11 12

Not all boomerangs come back. Australian Aborigines use returning boomerangs to drive game like kangaroos into nets, and then use non-returning boomerangs to kill them.

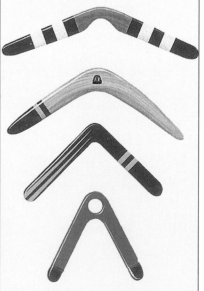

Landscapes of sand

On the north coast of Brazil, in the rolling dunes, people collect sand of every color imaginable. Artists meticulously fill bottles with grains of different colors, using needles, spatulas, and endless patience to create complicated pictures and landscapes in the sand.

Make a club sandwich, a meal between two slices of bread!

First toast the bread. Smear one slice with mayonnaise and cover it with slices of cold roast chicken or turkey. Add a leaf of lettuce, some slices of crisp bacon, and a few pieces of tomato. Finally top it with the other piece of toasted bread. The club is an American classic.

French children play this game. Why not try it?

Each player needs:
6 matches (for the legs and eyes), 1 round piece of potato and 2 whole cloves (for the nose), 1 piece of macaroni (for the tail), 2 triangles of cardboard (for the ears), 1 big potato (for the body) and 1 small one (for the head).

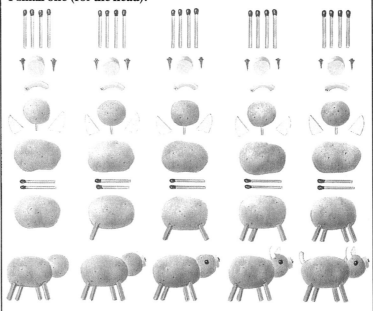

Each player throws a numbered die in turn.
The number you roll helps you to put together your pig.
6 = tail, 5 = body or head, 4 = nose, 3 = eye, 2 = ear, 1 = leg.
The first to make a pig wins the game!

A Japanese meal

The Japanese chop their meat, fish, and vegetables into small cubes, which are easy to pick up and eat with chopsticks.

Soy sauce

Tofu (bean curd)

They prepare a lot of fish raw, soaking it in vinegary sauces. Then they eat it dipped in soy sauce mixed with green mustard. Rice and green tea accompany all meals.

Japanese cakes

Presentation is important in Japanese cooking. Food is eaten off of beautiful plates of lacquered wood, colorful ceramics, or plastic. Cooks take courses to learn how to arrange food and decorate plates.

■ Glossary

Abacus: a Chinese invention to help you add quickly. Some shop assistants in China still use this old calculator.

Aborigines: the first Australians, who came over from Asia in prehistoric times. Many still live in the bush as their ancestors did.

Archipelago: a large group of islands.

Arctic: the area north of 60 degrees latitude, including parts of Canada, Alaska, Russia, and Scandinavia.

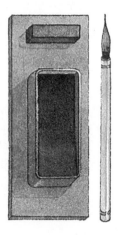

Cartography: the art and science of drawing maps. Early cartographers were not able to get accurate information about unknown parts of the world, so their maps did not show the world as it really is.

Civilization: the culture and way of life a group of people develop over centuries.

Conquistadores: Spanish conquerors who overcame the Indians of South and Central America in the 16th century. Their leaders were Cortés, who conquered the Aztecs in Mexico, and Pizarro, who destroyed the Incas in Peru.

Culture: describes the way of life, ideas, customs, and traditions of a group of people.

Custom: something that is regularly done by a group of people; a habit or tradition.

Dalai Lama: a living god and spiritual leader of the Tibetans. Since China invaded Tibet in 1950, the Dalai Lama has lived in exile in India.

Dreamtime: stories told by the Australian Aborigines for many generations about the beginning of the world and the adventures of the first people.

Earthquake: a violent shaking of the Earth's surface, caused by huge movements along the fault lines in the Earth's crust. Certain parts of the world suffer frequent earthquakes, such as Japan, the West Coast of the United States, and parts of Asia.

Equator: an imaginary line running around the middle of the Earth. Near the equator the climate is hot and sticky, and summer and winter have almost the same weather.

Ethnic: having to do with a group of people who share the same origins, language, or culture.

Exile: when people are forced to leave the country they call home.

Favela: a run-down district of a town or city where poor people live, often in rough and crowded conditions.

Gaucho: cowboy of South America. *Gauchos* ride the *pampas* (grasslands), rounding up cattle.

Immigrant: someone who comes to settle in a country permanently.
Indigenous: the people and plants that grow and live in an area and were not brought from elsewhere.
Irrigate: to water the fields artificially instead of waiting for rain. This can be done with canals, electric pumps, sprinklers, reservoir water, and even by changing the course of nearby rivers.

Kayak: an Inuit canoe made of sealskin stretched over a frame of driftwood and made for one passenger. *Umiaks* are larger boats that can carry six or eight people and are often used by hunting parties.

Lagoon: a calm lake of salty water, separated from the open sea by a sandbank or coral reef. This calm water makes fishing easier for coastal fishermen.

Machete: a broad, heavy knife that people in Central America and the West Indies use as a tool and a weapon.
Mosque: a Muslim church. Muslims pray here every day, getting down on their knees facing Mecca, and bowing low in homage to their holy city.

Nomads: wandering people who have no fixed home. Nomads usually live in tents that they pack up and carry with them on the backs of their horses or camels, or on their own backs.
North Pole: the most northerly point on Earth, at the icy center of the Arctic Circle. The South Pole is at the other extreme of the Earth, in the middle of the freezing Antarctic continent.

Oasis: a small paradise in the desert. In some parts of the Sahara, springs of water flow near the surface, creating green islands in the desert.
Outback: the Australian bush, ranging from scrub to arid desert. Kangaroos roam the outback, where the few people live on huge farms called stations.

Polo, Marco: an Italian traveler who visited China in the 13th century. He returned to Venice full of fantastic tales of the great civilizations of the East. One of the novelties he brought back to Italy with him was pasta.

Savanna: the grasslands of Africa, where some of the largest mammals live. There are few trees and little shade. The savanna is similar to the grasslands of the American prairies, the Argentine *pampas,* and the Russian steppes.
Siesta: in countries of southern Europe where the weather is hot, people take a rest, or *siesta,* after lunch when the sun is high in the sky. After an hour or two, they get up again and continue working.
Steppe: a flat, grassy plain in eastern Europe, Russia, and Siberia where no trees grow. It is cold in winter.

Tradition: customs, beliefs, and lifestyles that are passed down from generation to generation in a culture.
Tundra: a huge, flat area in the Arctic where the subsoil (the soil below the surface) is always frozen and there are no trees.

There are many things you can do to learn more about the way people live around the world and in your own area. Here are some ideas:

Join in the fun! People from all around the world have brought their traditions and celebrations with them to new places. Depending upon where you live, you may be able to join in on some of these. Here are a few ideas:

• **Cinco de Mayo** is celebrated on May 5 in Mexican communities with parades, food, and fun. It marks the day Mexicans defeated French troops at the Battle of Puebla.

• **Chinese New Year** falls between January 21 and February 19. It includes parades, fantastic feasts, setting off firecrackers, and religious ceremonies.

• **A Native American Powwow** may last one day, a week, or more. At a powwow, Native Americans celebrate with dancing, food, exhibiting arts and crafts, and wearing traditional tribal clothing.

• **Bastille Day** is celebrated by the French on July 14. It is like the Fourth of July in the United States, with firecrackers, parades, and other traditional festivities.

Try eating a new kind of ethnic food. Next time you eat out with friends or family, try a Vietnamese, Chinese, Afghan, Indian, or Mexican restaurant. Or try cooking an ethnic meal at home with the help of an adult. A librarian can help you find a good cookbook.

Write to a pen pal from another country. Ask friends and relatives if they know anyone who might like to exchange letters with you. You could also ask your librarian for resources, or ask an adult to help you find a pen pal on the Internet.

Ask your parents if they'd like to **host an exchange student.** Children from many different countries travel to other countries to live for a few months or a year and go to school. These students usually live with a family in the country they visit.

Listen to music. Many cultures have a special kind of music that is all their own. Your library may have tapes or CDs that you can borrow.

Read, read, read! You can travel anywhere in the world with a book.

Attend a performance. Performers from many different countries dance, drum, and sing their way all around the world.

Visit culture centers and history museums. Many of these can be found in smaller towns as well as in large cities.

The entries in **bold** refer to whole chapters on the subject.

A

Abacus, 43, 70
Aborigine, 48, 64, 68, 70
Afghanistan, 33, 60–61
Africa, The Sahara Desert, 24, Grasslands and rainforests, 25, The Tuareg people, 26, The Sahara Desert, 27, Villages in Central Africa, 28, School days and market days, 29, Days of celebration, 30, Modern cities, 31; *see also* 4, 52, 60–61
Alaska, 14, 57
Amazon, The Amazon River, 23; *see also* 17
Amsterdam, 7, 60
Andes, Home to descendants of the Incas, 19; *see also* 17
Arctic, 70
    Circle, 5, 56
    Ocean, 34, 60–61
Argentina, 16, 19, 60
Armenia, 34, 61
Asia is the world's most populated continent, 32, Many different landscapes, 33, Russia, shared between Europe and Asia, 34; *see also* 4, 10, 60–61
Atlantic Ocean, 4, 5, 10, 16, 19, 24, 60
    Coast, 16
Australasia, Islands in the Ocean: Australasia, 48, 60–61
Australia, 49, Long sandy beaches, wide open spaces, 50, Farmers in the outback, 51, 60–61
Austria, 8, 60–61
Azerbajan, 34
Aztecs, 16, 18

B

Baltic Sea, 4, 5
Bamboo, 45, 54
Bastille Day, 8, 72
Beijing, 44, 46, 47, 60
Belarus, 34
Belgium, 8, 60–61
Bengal, 32
Black Sea, 4
Bolivia, 19, 60
Boomerang, 68
Borneo, 32
Brahmanputra, 37
Brazil, 20–21; *see also* 19, 22, 60
Buddhism, 32, 43
Bulgaria, 8, 60–61

C

Camel, 26, 32, 33, 36, 64, 65, 71
Canada, 11; *see also* 12, 14, 60
Cape Horn, 17
Caribbean Sea, 17
Carpathian Mountains, 5
Cartography, 32, 70
Caspian Sea, 4
Cassava, 28, 29
Caucasus Mountains, 34
Central America, South and Central America, 16, 60
Chapatti, 37
Cheese, 9
Chile, 19, 60
Chili peppers, 29
China, One quarter of all the people are Chinese, 44, Chinese, but also Tibetan, Mongol, and Manchu, 45, Rice or noodles with meals, tea any time, 46, Most Chinese live in the countryside, 47; *see also* 32, 33, 60–61
Chinese
    food, 46
    inventions, 70
    New Year, 72
Chopsticks, 41
Christianity, 32
Christmas, 8
Cinco de Mayo, 72
Civilization, 4, 70
Coconut, 54, 55
Colombia, 19, 60
Congo, 30, 31, 60–61
    River, 31
Conquistadores, 16, 18, 70
Continental climate, 5

Cowboy, 10; *see also gaucho*
Cyclone, 55
Cyrillic alphabet, 35
Czech Republic, 5, 60

D

Dalai Lama, 45, 70
Day of the Dead, 18
Denmark, 9, 60–61

E

Earthquake, 18, 40, 70
Easter, 8
Ecuador, 19, 60
Egypt, 60–61, 64
England, 6, 9, 60
Equator, 5, 23, 25, 52, 70
Eskimos, *see* Inuit
Estonia, 34, 60
Europe—a small, crowded continent, 4–5, Homes for hot weather, homes for the cold, 6, A world of variety, 7, Costumes, celebrations, and customs, 8, Every country has its own foods, 9; *see also* 10, 60–61
European Union (E.U.), 4

F

Finland, 5, 60–61
France, 5, 7, 9, 60–61
French Guiana, 19, 60
Futon, 41

G

Ganges, A sacred river, 39; *see also* 37
Gaucho, 17, 22, 70
Germany, 8, 9, 60–61
Gobi Desert, 32
Great Britain, 5, 7, 8, 9, 60–61
Great Lakes, 14
Great Wall of China, 45
Greece, 6, 9, 60–61
Greenland: a land of ice in the far north, 56, The winter evenings are long and dark, 57, 60
Gulf of Mexico, 14
Guyana, 19, 60

H

Halloween, 13
Hanukkah, 8
Hawaii, 14
Himalayas, 32, 33, 36
Hinduism, 32, 39
Hokkaido, 40
Honshu, 40
Huang River, 45
Hungary, 5, 8, 60–61

I

Iceland, 4, 60
Iguacu Falls, 16
Incas, 16, 19, 23
India: a land of colors and contrasts, 36, The monsoon, 37, An Indian wedding, 38, The Ganges, 39; *see also* 33, 65
Indian Ocean, 36, 61, 68
Indians, 10, 16, 19; *see also* Native American, Navaho
Inuit, Greenland, 56, The winter evenings are long and dark, 57, Teams of dogs drag sleds, 58, How to make an igloo? 59
Iran, 33, 60–61
Ireland, 5, 60–61
Islam, 32
Israel, 33, 60–61
Istanbul, 33
Italy, 7, 9, 60–61

J

Japan: a string of more than 3,000 islands, 40, Ancient customs, 41, The busy streets of Tokyo, 42, Spectacular kite fights, 43; *see also* 60–61, 66
Jerusalem, 33, 60
Judaism, 32

K

Kalahari Desert, 25
Kangaroo, 49
Kayak, 57, 71
Kazakhstan, 34, 61
Kerala, 36
Khirgiz, 33

Kimono, 41
Koala, 49
Kyushu, 40

L Lagoon, 53, 71
Languages, 7, 11, 16, 35, 64
Laos, 33, 60–61
London, 48, 60

M Machete, 28, 71
Madagascar, 52, 60–61
Maize, 19, 28
Map of the World, 60–61
Maple, 11
Markets, 7, 29
Marsupial, 49
Martial Arts, 66
Mayas, 16, 18
Mediterranean, 4, 5, 7
Mexico, 18; see also 14, 16, 19, 60
Mexico City, 18, 60
Mongolia, 34, 35, 45, 60–61
Monsoon, 37; see also 32
Moscow, 34, 61
Mosque, 33, 45, 71
Mount Fuji, 40

N Native Americans, 10, 12, 72
Navaho Indians, 14
Netherlands, 6, 7, 9, 60–61
New York, a jungle of skyscrapers, 15; see also 48
Nomads, 24, 26, 33, 35, 45, 71
North America, 10, Canada, 11, 60–61
North Pole, 5, 71
North Sea, 4
Norway, 5, 60–61
Nossy-Be, 52, 53

O Oasis, 45, 71
Outback, 51, 71

P Pacific Ocean, 12, 14, 19, 40, 60–61
Coast, 14, 15
Pakistan, 33, 60–61
Pampas, 17, 22
Panama Canal, 19
Paraguay, 19, 60
Pasta, 9, 46, 71
Patagonia, 17
Peru, Cuzco, the former Inca capital, 22; see also 16, 19, 60
Poland, 5, 60–61
Polo, Marco, 46, 71
Polynesia, 48
Portugal, 9, 60
Pygmies, 30, 65

R Rainforest, 23, 25
Rajasthan, 36, 38, 65
Ramadan, 8
Rio de Janeiro, 20, 21
Russia, shared between Europe and Asia, 34; see also 4, 35, 61

S **Sahara Desert,** The Sahara Desert, 24, The Tuareg people, 26, The Sahara Desert is their home, 27
San Francisco, 15
São Paulo, 21
Sari, 37
Savanna, 25, 71

Scandinavia, 6, 8
School, 13, 26, 29, 44, 51
Seal, 57, 58
Shikoku, 40
Shintoism, 43
Siberia, From icy Siberia to the deserts of Mongolia, 35; see also 32, 34, 57
Siesta, 7, 71
Slavery, 20
Slovakia, 5
Slums, 21, 71; see also favelas
South America, South and Central America, 16, From tropical beaches to the windswept tip of Tierra del Fuego, 17, The Andes are home to descendants of the Incas, 19, Brazil takes up half of South America, 20; see also 24, 60
Soviet Union, 34, 61
Spain, 7, 8, 60
Spices for flavoring food, 55
Steppes, 32, 34, 71
Sugarcane, 20, 54
Sushi, 41
Suzhou, 46
Sweden, 8, 60–61
Switzerland, 9, 60–61

T Taj Mahal, 33
Tea, 46
Temperate climate, 5
Teotihuacan, 18
Tiananmen Square, 44
Tibet, 33, 45
Tierra del Fuego, 16, 17
Tokyo, The busy streets of Tokyo, 42; see also 40
Toltecs, 18
Tortilla, 18
Trans-Siberian Express, 35
Tropical Islands, 52–53, Bananas, coconuts, and sugarcane thrive, 54, Spices for flavoring food, 55
Tropic of Cancer, 52
Tropic of Capricorn, 52
Tuareg people, 26, The Sahara Desert is their home, 27; see also 64
Tundra, 34, 71
Turkey, 32, 33, 60–61

U Ukraine, 34, 61
Union of Soviet Socialist Republics (USSR), 34, 61; see also Russia
United States, Fifty states, 12, Children in the U.S., 13, In the U.S., everything is big, 14, New York, 15; see also 34, 48
Uruguay, 19, 60

V Vanilla, 55
Venezuela, 17, 19, 60
Vietnam, 33, 60–61
Vladivostok, 34

W Wailing Wall, 33
Washington, George, 15
Watermelon, 31
White House, 15
World map, 60–61

Y Yangtze River, 33, 45, 46
Yom Kippur, 8

Z Zaire, see Congo
Zeus, 4